CORPORATE DHARMA

HUMAN VALUES AT WORK

KAMALRUKH JAL BARIA

This book is dedicated to my beloved parents,

who have been my everything in my life.

My best friends, my loving gurus, my very life breath.

I also dedicate this book to

my guru in my corporate life, Mr. Syamal Gupta,

Former Director Tata Sons Limited,

one of the Lord's finest creations.

There will never be another like him!

Contents

Contents

Contents

Acknowledgements

The debt that I owe to my parents can never be repaid. Mum and Dad, from your divine heavenly abode, I know you continue to watch over every endeavour of mine and that this book too has your blessings. You taught us everything we know today and made us what we are today.

I will always be at a total loss of words when it comes to thanking Mr. Syamal Gupta. Like a true guru, he guided me at every step of my career. I feel his constant presence even after he has departed. When confused, I simply ask myself how would Mr. Gupta act in this situation, and I find my answers. Most of the stories in this book are inspired by Mr. Gupta. I was singularly lucky to be at the feet of such a great master for over 30 years of my life.

To Mr. Partha Sarkar, Former Managing Director, Tata Finance Limited, I owe deep gratitude for teaching me some of the most invaluable lessons in life. A leader so lofty and yet so humble and caring in every way! To have been able to work with Mr. Sarkar was indeed a divine blessing.

My teammates Anuradha and Pramila have helped me bring out this book in more ways than one. Patiently listening to the stories, encouraging me all along, typing out the entire manuscript, guiding me on the publishing part, are but a few areas where they have been with me in this journey of getting the book ready.

To all my former colleagues and friends in life, I owe a whole lot of gratitude for they helped shape me. Through the myriad of experiences that we shared together, many of the stories in this book were made possible.

Author's Note

Dear Readers,

After completing my M.Com. (Master of Commerce) Degree from the Bombay University, I worked as a lecturer for 3 years, teaching the undergraduate students at a Commerce college in Mumbai.

In 1990, I acquired my MMS (Master of Management Studies) Degree from the Narsee Monjee Institute of Management Studies (NMIMS), Mumbai University.

Straight from the campus, I joined Tata Exports Limited (now Tata International Limited) as a Management Trainee. I moved within the Tata Group of companies for the next 10 years.

In 1991 I moved on to Bangalore as a part of the team that set up Tata BP Solar Limited, India's first fully solar company in the private sector.

After 2 years at Tata BP, it was my great privilege to set up the Renewable Energy Finance Department in Tata Finance Limited. This was a first in India, infact a first in this part of the globe.

I moved then to work with Mr. Syamal Gupta, Former Director Tata Sons, on global strategy for the Tata Group.

Before I finally put down my pen for the Tata Group as an employee, I set up Human Resource Development in Tata International Limited.

As per my career plan, after 10 years with the Tata Group, 10 most wonderful years, in August 2000, I moved on to set up my first firm Synergy Management Consultants. Synergy Management works with a select basket of corporate clients, helping them in their people initiatives. In 2008, I founded The Hermitage, my second firm. The Hermitage works on a wider canvass which includes training programmes for the student world as well.

This book is a compilation of the leadership lessons that I was privileged to receive from the best of leaders in the House of Tatas.

Right from my days as a Management Trainee I was blessed to work with marvellous leaders; leaders of sterling character, leaders whom you would want to look up to and emulate.

Corporate Dharma is a tribute to all those who taught me how corporate life, just like our personal life, is what we make of it.

The 5 basic human values of truth, righteous conduct, love, peace and non-violence are universal. They permeate our personal and professional lives.

Where truth prevails, the work environment generates tremendous positive energy. People love coming to work and contribute generously and whole-heartedly.

Actions are guided by righteousness in such an environment. Because there is love in the heart, trust is the outcome. Teams thrive on mutual trust.

It is a joy to be working in such an organisation. People pursue goals and ambitions with the spirit of healthy competition and friction is dealt with in the most mature fashion, for non-violence is an enhanced expression of love in the heart.

The wise ones teach us, "Practise any one value and the rest will follow." I chose the path of love.

This book hopes to reinforce the belief and faith of the corporate world, in dealing with people and driving results the humane way.

The names of the seniors are shared so as to highlight their greatness. Though always very humble inspite of all their achievements, each of them is a towering personality.

Where required, I have masked the names of the people featuring in my stories so as not to cause any hurt to anybody.

All stories shared are my true experiences.

I do hope that you find these stories inspiring.

Please feel free to share your feedback with me on kbaria@gmail.com. You may like to visit www.thehermitage.in to get to know more about Synergy Management and The Hermitage.

With love,
Kamalrukh

CHAPTER ONE

Are you alright

One afternoon, my senior, the Managing Director of Tata International Limited, Mr. Syamal Gupta, called me to his room. He looked very concerned.

"Are you alright? "He asked.

"Yes, I am fine" I responded.

"Are you sure you are fine?"

"Of course, I am fine. Thank-you"

"Oh, but I am very concerned. Are you really sure that you are fine?" he persisted,

"Look, I told you I am fine. Why do you keep asking again and again? Do I know better or do you know better?" I fumed.

This little outburst of mine seemed to delight him. With a mischievous glee in his eyes, he said, "Please carry on with your work. You have now made my day."

"What was all this about? You called me only for this?" I asked.

"Oh, you see, there wasn't one good fight out of you since the morning, so I was concerned" he responded.

"You make it sound as if I come to work just to fight with you!" I could not figure out what Mr. Gupta was up to.

I walked back towards my workstation telling myself, "What a waste of 5 minutes!"

I thought this brief interlude was an interruption in the busiest part of my day, when I was involved in solving some vexing issues.

Why would the boss want to do this? Did he have nothing else to do? Was he just having fun at my expense?

After this self-perceived waste of 5 minutes, when I returned to my desk, I suddenly discovered a different perspective to the issues on hand. My work flowed faster.

I was now able to smile at the entire episode, my anger vanished. I soon realised that Mr. Gupta was appreciative of my independent thinking, which was often very different from his way of looking at things.

Mr. Gupta never tried to stifle independent thought. In fact, he encouraged us to think differently and gave us platforms to voice our independent views courageously.

Note on LBOs

Let me share an instance here, to show you how he did this.

Tuesday morning meetings, as we knew them, were meetings attended by all senior level leaders of the company, Vice Presidents and General Managers (VPs & GMs).

One Tuesday after the morning meeting, a VP came up to me (I was a Management Trainee at that time in Tata Exports Ltd.) and asked me "What is an LBO?" I explained Leverage Buy Outs to him. He asked me to put up a one page note to him, with examples of LBOs, by the evening.

I was new around the company, so I went about looking for a library with HBRs (Harvard Business Review magazines). With some help I located a treasure trove of HBRs neatly standing in a glass bookcase, just outside the Managing Director's room, in fact in his secretary's room. It was lunch time, and no one was around. I started browsing through various editions and pulled out a few.

"Just what do you think you are doing here, young lady?" came a thundering voice over my shoulders. It was the Managing Director, Mr. Syamal Gupta. I wasn't aware that he had walked up to me.

"I am just pulling out a few HBRs for reference because I have to put up a one-pager on LBOs for the VP by this evening," I responded.

He asked, "Do you know this is my personal collection?"

To which I responded, "Oh, I am sorry. I asked for reference material, HBRs in particular and I was directed here by someone. May I please read these?"

He agreed saying, "Alright but make sure you put them back exactly at the same place from where you pulled them out."

Now I was in deeper trouble, "I cannot do that because I didn't know that there was an order to it. I was just pulling out whatever interested me."

He smiled and said I could leave them on his secretary's desk, once I was through with my research and that she would put them all back. On his way back to his chamber he paused and said "And let me also have a copy of that one page note that you are preparing."

CHAPTER THREE

Read and discuss with me

While I was going through the HBRs Mr. Gupta came up to me again saying "You seem to like reading."

"Oh yes, at my management institute, NMIMS, we have a fantastic library which is a great learning resource to stay up to date. However, unfortunately here I do not find that kind of support," I responded.

"Well, you can come here in your lunch time to read. You could read anything from my collection here but on one condition. You must sit here and read and not take away any material from here" he offered.

I agreed instantly and thanked him. He immediately added, "There is another condition to it as well. At the end of your reading, you must discuss what you read, with me." I was game for it.

The next afternoon, after quickly finishing lunch with my teammates, I headed straight to my resource room.
I read a part of an article in an HBR for 15 minutes and boldly knocked on Mr. Gupta's door. He asked me what I had read. I told him.

He did not appear pleased with what I shared. "That is all what the author says. You tell me what you think about what the author says" he said. I was always one to speak up. I needed no second invitation. Inspite of knowing that the authors in HBRs are great management gurus who write after elaborate research, I still went ahead confidently to share what I thought about what I had read.

Next day, I read more of the same article and then I went up to Mr.Gupta and said, "I was wrong in my perception yesterday. Today I read a few more pages of the article and now what I think is ...."

He never made me feel stupid. On the contrary his probing questions made me delve deeper into what I was reading. Reading was no longer just reading to know. Reading now became reading to analyse, to apply, to learn and to share.

Oh, I must tell you, my dear readers, that when at the end of the first evening I handed over the one- pager to the VP, with a copy showing to the Managing Director, the VP was mad at me. I learnt that the Managing Director had asked him about LBOs in that morning's Tuesday meeting and when he said he did not know about it, he was told that he must, by the evening, learn about LBOs.

CHAPTER FOUR

Send a fax message

Talking about my Management Trainee days makes me shudder to think about some of the guffaws I have made.

I was always early to reach office. I used to believe that I was the first one to arrive each day, until one day I discovered that it was the Managing Director, Mr. Syamal Gupta who would already be present in his chamber much before I arrived. One such early morning when I was settling down at my desk, Mr. Gupta emerged from his room. He seemed to be looking for someone to help him. Noticing me, he came up to me and asked, "Do you know how to send a fax message?"

"Yes, I do. Do you want to send one? Please give it to me, I shall send it for you." Like every fresher, I was keen to impress my seniors.

He seemed pleased and said, "Please come with me."

As I followed him to his room, I said to myself, 'Thank God that out of my own interest, I learnt how to use the fax machine last evening from the fax operator. Otherwise, this morning, the Managing Director would have thought that these MBAs do not even know how to send a fax message.'

Mr. Gupta courteously saw me seated in my chair and then went across his desk and took his seat. He held out four pages to me.

The four pages were full of numbers, tables and graphs. He told me that a particular associate of the company based abroad, was about to get into a meeting to close a large business deal, for which he urgently needed some information from our side. At that point in time, those four pages were very crucial, and the business associate was eagerly waiting by the fax machine at his end, so that he could enter the meeting to take up the discussion on our behalf.

Having explained the big picture to me, Mr. Gupta handed over those four sheets and the fax number to which the message had to be transmitted.

Eager to please the Big Boss, I rushed to the fax room and placed the papers correctly and dialled the number and saw the first sheet going through correctly. Very pleased with myself, I moved back to my desk assuming that the remaining 3 pages will be relayed automatically, just as I had seen it happen the previous evening.

After 10 minutes Mr. Gupta was back at my desk asking, "Has the message gone through?"

"Yes, I saw it go" I replied enthusiastically.

He continued "Shall we check please, because I just received a call from our associate that he has received only one page."

"Oh, is that so?" I responded, "I saw the first page being relayed and I assumed that the rest would follow. Let me send it again" so saying I began to make a dash for the fax room.

He raised his hand to pause me and said, "It is too late now my child, that person is already into the meeting. Next time shall we ensure that we stand by the machine and see the whole message go through?"

I went pale. I could only manage to mutter "I am sorry".

Big business deal, crucial information, urgently required data!! Inspite of being shown the importance and urgency of the seemingly simple task of sending a fax message, I had messed it all up. The deal would be lost because a foolish MBA did not do her job right.

But why did he not scold me for this apparent loss to the company? Maybe he was waiting for the Vice President, Human Resource and others to arrive in the office and then I may be fired and thrown out from my first job. Who will then employ me? I was shaken to my core.

Each time that morning when Mr. Gupta came out of his room towards my work area, my heart would beat louder. Is this it? Will I be fired now? Will he scold me in front of all and let all in the office know what a blunder I made? None of these dreaded thoughts fructified. All I went home with that day was, "Next time shall we ensure that we stand by the fax machine and see the whole thing go through."

Years later, when I had a good rapport with Mr. Syamal Gupta, I asked him whether he remembered this incident. His smile told me he did. "But then why did you not shout at me? Why did you not throw me out? Any ordinary person would have done it" I said. His response still rings in my ears. "How else were you to learn, my child?"

Here was a person who was willing to take a business beating of a big magnitude but was unwilling to give up on a young Management Trainee in whom he saw potential. Obviously, he was not an ordinary person.

CHAPTER FIVE

Golden words are repeated

When I was heading Renewable Energy Finance, in Tata Finance Limited, I was once working on a very tight schedule. I had to send out a proposal for a multi-crore deal within 3 hours. I worked at breakneck speed to arrive at a correct lease rental figure to quote. Even one paisa here and there could cause a big loss to the company. After some time my boss, the Managing Director of that company, Mr.Partha Sarkar, joined me at my desk and together we looked at varied scenarios.

Just when I would think I had arrived at the correct figure, Mr.Sarkar would show me why that wasn't the right figure and when he would suggest a figure, I would soon prove that figure wrong. This went on until 11.45 a.m. 12 noon was the deadline to send the proposal. Mr.Sarkar was then convinced that the lease rental he was proposing was the most beneficial one to the customer and to our company.

I asked him to leave me alone for 5 minutes so that I could run through my arguments peacefully to show him why I still did not agree. Promptly he got up and left. It took me just 5 minutes to realise that Mr. Sarkar was right and that the lease rental suggested by him was correct. I rushed to tell him that he was right. We managed to send out our proposal in time.

Later I asked him "When you knew that you were right and you also knew that we were running out of time, and we could have lost out on this deal, why did you not prevail upon me?"

Once again, I heard the same words that I had heard in my Management Trainee days. "How else were you to learn? I have full confidence on your capabilities and respect your commitment to the organisation."

'What makes these leaders tick thus?' I wondered.

CHAPTER SIX

Read the small print

I was very blessed to get to learn from the best. In my Management Trainee days, I used to stay back late in the office and read up a lot of work-related files. This used to help me understand and learn a whole lot of things that happened in the world of commerce and trade.

On one such evening, our Director-Finance, Mr. Hoshie Malgham who also happened to be working late that evening, noticed me sitting all alone in my department pouring over files. He requested me to join him in his room.

That evening, he shared with me a whole lot of his experiences related to Letters of Credit (LOC). He prevailed upon me how important it was to read the small print in LOCs. The stories he shared were real eye openers.

CHAPTER SEVEN

Who made this mistake

That was also the time when Tata Exports Limited (TEL) was setting up a joint venture with BP Solar of UK. Those days the government exerted strong control over corporates. A multitude of applications had to be made, a plethora of forms had to be filled up, and a large number of permissions and licences had to be obtained. There were 3 major entities involved, TEL, BP Solar and Tata BP (TBP), the new company sought to be incorporated. The different applications had to be signed and sent out under varied names and designations of individuals drawn from these entities. Moreover, some individuals held positions in differing capacities, in more than one of these entities.

The deadline for submission of one of the major applications was close at end. I was assisting the Company Secretary, Mr. S. H. Rajadhyaksha, in preparing this document. I was new and did not know most of the people under whose names and designations I was preparing the applications.

In all my ignorance I prepared the covering letter to this application with the incorrect designation under the signatory's name. I even got the signatory to sign it and my Company Secretary made sure that the Director-Finance, Mr. Hoshie H. Malgham was on the flight to Delhi that evening to submit the application the next morning.

After reaching Delhi, Mr. Malgham started going through the

documents. He was always very thorough and nothing missed his eye. The deadline for submission was looming large and to make matters worse he was saddled with a document incorrectly signed. Those days the means of communication were limited. He called up the Company Secretary and somehow between the two of them they salvaged the situation.

Upon his return to Mumbai, Mr. Malgham came up to the Company Secretary wanting to know who had made that mistake. My heart was thudding loudly. I expected that soon that tirade will be directed towards me. But my Company Secretary kept on repeating that it was his mistake and that he should have checked the documents thoroughly before handing them over to the Director-Finance. Mr. Malgham insisted on knowing the name, but the Company Secretary stood his ground taking the entire blame onto his shoulders.

Afterwards I went up to the Company Secretary and apologised once again and asked him why he did not name me. "Remember this lesson. Whenever you delegate a task, you do not delegate accountability. You will still be accountable for its outcome. What I said was correct. I should have checked thoroughly. It was my mistake."

We all learn from mistakes, but we need such wonderful leaders to help bring the lessons home.

Maria joins the Renewable Energy Finance team

The year was 1993-94. I was back from the USA having had some very successful meetings at the World Bank and with several other agencies.

At that time there was a line of credit from the World Bank available to India for financing renewable energy projects and Tatas decided to use it to give a fillip to renewable energy in the country. It was my job in Tata Finance, to design financing models and to on-lend funds to those wanting to set up renewable energy projects.

I called up my Vice President Human Resource (VP-HR) requesting his help to build my team. I asked for MBAs in Finance and /or Marketing. Renewable energy knowledge would be an added advantage but in those days this kind of combination was difficult to find. Within 20 minutes, the VP-HR called to say that he had located a lady internally and she was on her way from the suburban office to my office in town. I was thrilled. I did not expect to see my team falling in place so soon.

"Is she an MBA in Marketing?" I asked the VP-HR.

'No' came the response across the telephone line.

"MBA Finance like me? Great! We will talk a common language." I was very excited.

'No' was the response again.

"Then a renewable energy expert! Wow, I did not know that in our Finance company we had a renewable energy expert." My excitement was mounting.

"You seem to get me wrong each time." The VP-HR responded. "Maria is a B.A. in Sociology and has been with our company for over 10 years.

"That is great. Over 10 years in the Finance industry. That is excellent experience. Her experience will more than make up for her lack of qualifications." I added.

"You are again getting me wrong." The VP responded coolly. "She has been with us for over 10 years in the capacity of a secretary. She is currently my secretary. She has been promoted to an executive cadre, but I do not have a suitable opening in my department. You are looking for Executives. Take a look, otherwise I can always look outside the company for you."

I was never one to lose my cool easily. I certainly was not looking for a secretary and how can a secretary of 10 years be selling money as a product and that too for renewable energy systems!

I had already decided that Maria was not the right fit for my job. I planned to talk to her politely, offer her a cup of tea and send her back to her HR office in the suburbs.

Maria arrived soon and we got talking. Maria was a delight to meet. She was so upfront, so downright honest, so willing to learn and so pleasant a personality. Her giggles were the sweetest part of her personality.

I shared with Maria that there were 3 angles to the job, Finance, Marketing and Renewable energy. I first spoke about the Marketing angle of the job to which she responded by saying, "You are talking of selling money for renewable energy projects, but I have not sold even a pencil in my life. However, if you are willing to teach me, I am ready to learn."

Next, we discussed the Finance angle. Maria said, "This is a Finance company and I keep hearing debit and credit but I don't know what those terms mean. But if you are ready to teach me, I am willing to learn."

I shared about solar water heating systems and like on the earlier two occasions, this time too Maria giggled and then said, "All I know about solar energy is that, that fellow comes out in the sky each day and gives me light and warmth. But if you are ready to teach me, I am ready to learn."

I do not know what made me take to Maria. It was like an instant bond of love that was established between us. I said, "Maria, give me 6 months. In 6 months, I will teach you everything I know about all the three angles of our work. At the end of 6 months if you tell me that this is not quite your cup of tea and you were happier being a secretary, I will let you go without a grudge. You too must be fair to me. If at the end of 6 months I find you are not shaping up, we must part ways amicably." The bargain was struck. We started working together.

6 months later, Maria had worked miracles.

When it came to reading, interpreting and projecting the financial statements of our prospective clients, Maria could match any Chartered Accountant.

I always thought that Mumbai was a very power-happy place with no power cuts and with uninterrupted power supply. Who then would want an alternate source of energy in such a place? My Maria opened out a huge market for solar water heating in the hospital segment in the city.

When Maria went to inspect the solar collectors which we would eventually fund, she would most of the times end up infuriating the vendors. The reason would be that she would reject all the hundreds of collectors shown to her, on the grounds that they were painted by hand. This meant that such collectors would not function perfectly for the full tenure of the lease, which was 10 years. Maria developed this knack of being able to tell this with her naked eyes.

Soon Maria built a thriving business segment in solar water heating for the Company, ensuring a win-win for the lessee organisation, the vendor and our company.

Maria was a huge asset on the team. Eventually the team expanded and Maria continued to guide me and others through her experience at handling varied equations at work. Varied tricky situations were always easy to tackle because of Maria on our team.

CHAPTER NINE

Delay in Maria starting work

I recall that once it was decided that Maria would be joining the Renewable Energy Finance (REF) team, she informed me that she would be able to start work only after 2 weeks. Her brother from the USA was visiting and she wanted to spend time with family. I said I was willing to wait, for if I was in her place, I too would want to be with family at such time.

"But then my salary will begin to be debited to the REF department immediately" she said. "No problem, I will take the debit" was my response.

When it was time for Maria to join work, her mother took seriously ill. Unfortunately, Maria lost her mother. Then it was decided that as per her mother's last wish Maria would get married quickly in a church before her siblings left for the USA again.

Finally, Maria was able to begin work after about 45 days. The rest of the story is already told in the earlier pages of this book.

When I wondered aloud how Maria could perform to the level she did, she said the understanding and support that she received from the Company in her difficult times spurred her to give her best.

CHAPTER TEN

Gopal's desk

I am reminded of another story from my Tata Finance days. Once there was renovation to happen in my work area. My team of 3 and I were asked to shift to another area in the office for the interim period. This temporary arrangement gave us 3 desks together at one place and one desk slightly far from those 3.

I decided that I would sit along with my 2 new management trainees and Maria could take the other desk. I thought this arrangement was perfect. I needed to parallelly guide my management trainees whereas Maria was capable of working independent of me.

Maria did not appear happy with this arrangement. I discovered that what pained her was that I had asked her to occupy a desk which was previously used by the office peon. She was not comfortable sitting at a peon's desk. I offered to switch places with her if that made her happy and she was game for it. She even offered to guide the 2 new management trainees with their work.

After 2 days Maria came up to me saying, "If you still want me to take this desk, I can do so. Now this desk looks different."

CHAPTER ELEVEN

Increment in basic salary

One morning, my boss, Mr. Partha Sarkar, Managing Director, Tata Finance Ltd. called me and gave me an envelope saying "Kamal, this is for you." I love surprises. "What is in it?" I asked. "It is a small increment in your salary, a small token to say Thank-you for all that you are doing for this company."

My first reaction was, "Are you going to give the same raise to my team as well? Without them I could have achieved nothing." From the look on his face, I could make out that he hadn't thought of it. I politely pushed the envelope on the table back to him, thanking him but at the same time expressing my inability to accept it. He pushed it back in my direction, requesting me to accept it and assuring me that my team too would be given the same reward. "Please if you could reward the team first and me last? That would really make me happy," I requested. He agreed and told me to leave the envelope behind.

CHAPTER TWELVE

Biggest idiot alive

As I came out of the Managing Director's room, my team of 3 which had gathered at his door, shouted a loud "Congratulations!" Then seeing that I had come out empty-handed, they thought they had let the cat out of the bag.

"He was supposed to give you something, didn't he do that?" They asked. "Yes, but I declined. He was very understanding and he is now to reward all of us equally" I explained.

My team was shocked. "You are the biggest idiot alive. Don't you understand that when a team leader is rewarded, it is acknowledgement of the entire team's work?"

I totally disagreed with them. "I am sorry to say that it is not me but you 3 who are biggest idiots alive. It is obvious that you were aware of this reward coming my way and yet the thought never crossed your minds that when all 4 of us had slogged together to bring in these spectacular results, why should only the team leader be rewarded?"

We could not conclude as to who was the biggest idiot alive.

CHAPTER THIRTEEN

Lonely at the top

We are all very appreciative of our juniors. We take great pride in sharing their achievements with others, but seldom do we go back to our bosses when they do a great job and say "Good job Boss!"

Whenever I have asked my participants, whom I now train as a corporate trainer, as to how many do this, the answer I get is, "Why must we do that? That's his job." Then why do we feel low when we are not appreciated by our bosses?

I once sent a thank-you message to my boss, the Managing Director of Tata Finance, Mr. Partha Sarkar, for immediately stepping in to help Maria on the personal front, at the time of a medical emergency. I got a response that said, "Thank you for your kind words. It is very lonely at the top."

CHAPTER FOURTEEN

I am with my boss

Vani, one of my junior colleagues at Tata Finance and I went on to Sunderbans for business. I was about 32 years of age then.

That night, I overheard my Vani's conversation with her grandmother. She was mentioning that her boss was with her. I got a little upset for I never felt I was a boss to my team, rather just a team member responsible for coordinating the team's efforts.

"Oh, you see someone scared my grandmother with stories of man-eating tigers prowling the Sunderbans so I had to say my boss is with me. That way my grandmother pictured an older and stronger person who would look after me" Vani explained.

Strange indeed, for eventhough my Vani appeared physically stronger than me and was 8 years younger, I always felt responsible for her wellbeing. Wonder what age and physical strength had to do with it.

CHAPTER FIFTEEN

Saw tigers in Sundarbans

Our visit to the Sunderbans was very eventful and yes, we did see those confirmed man-eating royal Bengal tigers. We were told that only a lucky few manage to see them.

Early morning when it was still dark, the helper of the guest house where we were staying came banging on our doors shouting "Baagh, baagh" which meant "Tiger, tiger". The previous night he had told us that on the other side of the fence there was a waterhole where the tigers came for a drink. He had promised to wake us, should he spot any tigers.

We quickly got on to the veranda facing the waterhole, trying hard to spot the tigers in the pitch dark morning. Then suddenly we saw 2 orange flames. A tiger's eyes have phosphorus and they shine in the dark, we were told. As our eyes got used to the dark, we slowly saw the whole shape of the tiger. Then there were many more pairs of flames and suddenly it was dawn. We couldn't believe our good fortune. We saw a horde of tigers sitting across the fence. They looked so regal, so proud and Oh! So beautiful!

I was full of joy upon my return to the office after this fantastic sight. I wanted to share this with everyone at work. That day I received a call from Mr. Gupta's office saying that he wished to meet me. I did not report to Mr. Gupta. Mr. Sarkar was my boss at Tata Finance but Mr. Gupta being far too senior in the Tata

Group, could not be disregarded. Eventhough, each time that we met, I would seldom agree with what Mr. Gupta had to tell me, I held Mr. Gupta in the highest esteem. Moreover, eversince my Tata Exports days as a Management Trainee, Mr. Gupta had stayed in touch with me and somehow seemed to know everything that I was up to at work.

I went across, eager to tell him about the sighting of the tigers.

Soon I discovered that Mr. Gupta was in no mood to listen to my story. He was visibly upset as to why I had ventured on such a dangerous trip. "Just because you are senior enough to decide where you can travel, does not give you the sanction to go on such risky escapades."

That day I was very upset with the kill-joy attitude of Mr. Gupta, though deep down I knew that he cared a whole lot for all of us and such rash actions on our part caused undue anxiety to him.

CHAPTER SIXTEEN

Jakarta airport

In 1995-96 I was at the Jakarta airport waiting for the local sponsors to pick me up. I was to participate in a Renewable Energy conference and to chair a session too.

A thin old man came up to me enquiring if I needed a taxi. I declined politely. The taxi driver stood across the lobby (which was not very large) and did not take his eyes off me. I was feeling uncomfortable under his unwavering watch. After a few minutes he again came up to me asking if I would like to hire a cab. I declined once again. When he offered a third time, I lost my cool and told him that even if I needed a cab, I would not hire him. Not paying any attention to my outburst, he again stood at the same spot across me, watching me.

I soon realised that Jakarta was a small airport and mine was the only flight to arrive at that time. The counters were all closing down. Quite close to where I was standing, was a currency exchange counter. I exchanged a few dollars for local currency. I even got a few coins which I thought I would need to make a local call.

Soon it was only the taxi driver and I left in the lobby with not another soul around. I had to somehow establish contact with the local sponsor. I desperately looked around for a local telephone. Having located one I searched for a slot to drop the coin but did not find any. The next moment I saw the taxi driver push in a phone card and then he asked me to talk. Unfortunately, the person on the other side spoke only Indonesian bhasha (the local language). I was forced to pass the receiver to the taxi driver. I gave him my name and asked him to enquire why there was nobody to receive me at the airport.

After concluding the call, the taxi driver told me that there was an apparent mix-up in the dates and that they were expecting me to arrive the next day. All the same they had requested me to take a cab and proceed to the hotel where the local hosts would receive me.

Fearful thoughts floated through my mind. He being a taxi driver could deceitfully be passing on such a message to me, I thought. It was obvious to him that this was my first visit to Indonesia and I knew nobody there nor did I speak their language. I had no option. There were no counters to book a taxi and there was nobody else around. He offered to drop me to my hotel and I agreed. Once out of airport terminal building, I observed that there was not a soul in sight and in the huge parking lot there was just one Honda car parked, which obviously belonged to this taxi driver. Once seated in his cab, my whole focus was on trying to remember the route he was taking. I was scared within though I tried not to let my face reveal it.

The taxi driver introduced himself as Eddy. He seemed very knowledgeable. He spoke about the education system, the law-and-order system, the state of the economy, the industries coming up etc. Eddy offered to show me around Jakarta and take me shopping. My whole being was screaming within "Just take me to my hotel. That's all I want."

Then after what felt like ages, I saw my hotel approaching. Eddy brought me to my hotel as promised.

That afternoon, I was at a loose end so I called Eddy and he took me sightseeing. I thanked him that evening as he dropped me back. I told him that starting from the next day I had a very busy schedule of work. He asked me when I was leaving and I told him.

On the day of my departure, I left from the hotel at 2 a.m. to take the flight back to Mumbai. As I stepped out of the hotel and moved towards the car, I felt that I was being watched. I got into the car and turned back. To my surprise, I saw Eddy quietly standing beside the hotel entrance. I went up to him "Eddy it is 2 a.m.! What are you doing here?"

"You see ma'am, 2 a.m. is not a safe hour here, for a lady to be alone in a car. Now that I see that there are 2 other gentlemen too with you in the car going to the airport, I shall go home peacefully"

"What would you have done if I was going alone Eddy?" I asked. In a very matter-of-fact manner, he replied "I would have followed your car."

What have I done to deserve so much love in this world? I have no answer. All of us are sent into this world blessed with this inexhaustible treasure trove of love. The more we give, the more the treasure trove gets filled. Eddy's treasure trove was truly inexhaustible.

CHAPTER SEVENTEEN

Mum's hospitalization

1995, the early part of the year was very difficult for me. While at work, one afternoon I received a call from my sister to say that our mother had been diagnosed with blockages in the arteries and needed an angioplasty on an emergency basis.

When I reached the hospital, another problem surfaced. The hospital said Mum had to undergo the angioplasty urgently, but one lakh rupees must be deposited with the hospital prior to that. We had never seen money of this quantum in our lives so far. I asked the hospital what if I could not organise that amount at so short a notice and the response that I received made my heart sink. I was told that the hospital was known to send away the patients even from the operation theatre door if the money was not received.

On one hand the hospital said Mum was critical and needed an angioplasty immediately, on the other hand they talked of sending away patients unattended, if they did not pay up the fees.

All I could do was to ring my then boss, the Managing Director of Tata Finance Ltd. Mr. Partha Sarkar. "Please take care of Mummy. That is your duty right now. Leave everything else to us," he advised.

Thanks to the Tatas, angioplasty happened as scheduled. Unfortunately, it was a big disaster. The main artery got cracked in the procedure. Now my mother's condition was worse than before. If she survived in this condition for 6 months, then she would need a bypass.

Mr. Sarkar understood my predicament, "The next time too when you need funds, don't go anywhere else. Please just come to us," he said.

My mother went through many downs in the ensuing months. At the end of 5 months, I took a bold call to go ahead with the bypass surgery. It was a huge risk, but I had no other option.

Not only did Tatas support me with the funds but a whole lot of my colleagues showed up to donate blood whenever my mother needed it.

Mum's recovery was not easy, but I had so much love all around me that I felt very supported and protected. While Mum was in the hospital, the Personnel Head of another Tata company that I had served earlier came to me with an envelope containing some cash saying that the Managing Director of that company had personally sent it and that I must keep it as I would need the funds for medicines, injections, etc. My current company, Tata Finance was taking very good care of me, even supporting me with funds, so I declined with gratitude.

Once I got my mother home, I was under very strict instructions from her surgeon not to allow any visitors at all near Mum. Her immunity was heavily compromised. Mr. Sarkar would call me every day to check on Mum and chat with me for about 40 minutes each day. As the conversation would continue, my mind would run wild and I would wonder how I would be able to cope if he asked me to resume work. I had nobody to help me look after my mother.

One day on one such telephonic call when I could bear the tension no longer, I asked, "Are you calling to check when can I resume work?"

"No Kamal. We do not want to see you anywhere close to the office until Mum has recovered," was the response I received.

Where do you find bosses like these? Where do you find companies and employers as my Tata group? They did not do it for me alone. They would do it for anyone in genuine need. Such are the beautiful people in these wonderful organisations.

Love alleviates and elevates. After the way the Tatas gave me back my mother, I had pledged to work for the Group lifelong. Even then I would not be able to repay the debt of what they had done for me.

CHAPTER EIGHTEEN

Writing a fax message 14 times

In 1997 I had moved into Mr. Gupta's office to work with him at the Group level. By then Mr. Gupta was also a Director on the Tata Sons Board of Directors. One day while we were both into a serious discussion, Mr. Gupta's secretary brought in his folder with his daily mail and messages which needed his attention. Mr. Gupta started going through the folder. He pulled out one fax message and passed it on to me saying, "Will you please send a suitable response to this, declining the meeting?" I glanced at the sheet of paper. It was a message from a dignitary from one of the African countries who was to lead a delegation from his country to India and was seeking a meeting with Mr. Gupta.

In response to the message, I wrote,
Dear Mr.--- We thank you for your fax message addressed to our Mr. Syamal Gupta seeking an appointment with him in course of your visit to India in the 2nd week of March. Much as Mr. Gupta would have loved to meet with you and your delegation, he will not be able to make it. We wish your delegation every success for your visit to India. With regards, Ms. Kamalrukh J. Baria

On my way to the fax room, I stopped by Mr. Gupta's room to double check that he was certainly not going to meet this delegation. His ways were pretty unpredictable. He would get us to decline and the next thing we would learn is that he was in a meeting with those very same people.

"You are surely not going to meet this delegation, right?" I asked.

"Yes, I am sure. But let me see what you wrote please" he said. I handed over the sheet to him.

"Surely you can write better than that" he quipped.

I thought it was a well written message and could not see any room for improvement, so I asked him what he wanted me to change, to which he responded "That I do not know. You see if I knew how to write, I would have written it myself. But please let me see the message before you send it out."

I redrafted and showed it to him but once again it was "Surely you can write better than this." He would simply not tell me where he wanted changes. If I asked, the answer was "If I knew how to write, I would have written it myself."

This went on and on. After 7 redrafts, I lost my cool and fumed, "You think I cannot write a good message. First of all, it is not my job to reply to your mail. Please give it to your secretary. She knows your style of writing."

He pushed the paper back to me pleading very sweetly, "You can't do this to me. If anyone can get it right in this office, I know it is you. Please give it another shot."

It was only on the 14th shot that he finally exclaimed, "See! I told you! Now let me see the first draft." He placed the first draft alongside the 14th one for me to read and asked me that if I were that African dignitary, which of the 2 drafts would sound better to me. I noticed that the only difference between the two drafts was that in the 14th one the words "he will not be able to make it" were replaced by "he is unable to make it."

My ego got a good bashing as I discovered that I was not so good at my writing abilities. The tone of the communication matters. A positive tone is always more welcome. I also learnt that however senior we may be in the corporate hierarchy, that does not imply that we know everything. There is so much to learn each day, from everybody.

Mr. Gupta had all the patience to bear with me for 14 redrafts but he did not give up on me, neither did he pay any heed to my tantrums and egoistic outbursts.

CHAPTER NINETEEN

British Chevening scholarship

In 1997 soon after I moved to work with Mr. Syamal Gupta, there was an announcement in the newspapers and on the Company's notice boards calling for applicants who wished to enrol for the Senior Executive Course (SEC) on Strategy at Manchester Business School (MBS). This was a 4-week programme and involved live projects. The British Chevening scholarship would cover the tuition fees for the programme. Only 8 scholarships, 4 per batch, were available for this course. The programme was to run for 2 separate batches in the year.

The application form had to be backed up by a detailed CV and 2 recommendations preferably from the work place. The shortlisted applicants needed to appear for an interview at the British Embassy in Delhi. My seniors prevailed upon me to apply. Tatas even had an internal round of interviews. As word went around the Tata Group that I was planning to apply for the scholarship, I was flooded with 13 seniors, some of them Managing Directors of their companies, sending across their letters of recommendation. It was tough to then choose only 2 out of the 13, which were all written so spontaneously for me and were all wrapped in so much love! I was granted the British Chevening Scholarship for the programme. Later I learnt that there were 7,000 applications for 4 scholarships for the first batch.

CHAPTER TWENTY

Tata London Ltd. Managing Director and the coat

I had some official work to complete in London so I visited our Tata Limited London office prior to going to Manchester. When I was about to leave from the office of the Managing Director of our London company, he gifted me with an overcoat saying it could get very cold in Manchester.

I said I was not to touch London on my return to Mumbai, so how then would I return the coat to him. He explained that the coat belonged to his wife and was in fact her favourite coat and he wanted me to have it. His wife had passed away just a few weeks ago due to cancer.

I was deeply touched. I still have the coat. I feel the warmth of love each time I wear it.

CHAPTER TWENTY-ONE

Mr. Gupta's call at MBS

One of the conditions for attending the Senior Executive Course at Manchester was that no one from the office would contact us while we were at the Business School. We were to be left undisturbed and allowed to focus fully on our studies.

One evening at the Manchester Business School, I received a phone call from my boss in Mumbai, Mr. Syamal Gupta. Those days there were no cell phones and all calls to us were routed through the telephone operator. I was scared that if the telephone operator reported this to my teachers, I would be asked to go back home immediately because it was a clear violation of one of the conditions of attending this course. Mr. Gupta assured me that he had only called to check if all was fine with me and he was certainly not going to talk work at all.

CHAPTER TWENTY-TWO

Please find someone else to work with

The course at Manchester was pretty hectic with classroom sessions running until late evenings and then there was project work. We had no break for 15 days straight.

On our first break we decided to drive up to Lake District. The place was like heaven on earth. Lake District was simply out of this world, with mother nature at her best and with people so soft- spoken and so helpful and kind. It was a great weekend.

I called Mr. Gupta to tell him that he needed to find someone else to work with, as I had decided to stay on in Lake District. Of course, I was kidding but Mr. Gupta very sweetly said "Do you like it there so much? Why don't you take a few days off after the programme and enjoy your stay and then come back?"

CHAPTER TWENTY-THREE

Insistence on carrying UK Pounds

I recall that a day prior to my departure for London, The Director- Finance, Mr. Hoshie Malgham, ran through all my arrangements for the Manchester Business School to make sure that I would be comfortable and safe at MBS for that one month.

He asked me if I had claimed foreign exchange from the office, to which I replied in the negative. Since I was going for studies and not for official work, I did not think it was right to claim foreign exchange from the office. Moreover, the scholarship included a stipend to help meet my local incidental expenses.

He insisted on the travel desk issuing some UK pounds to me. "Please keep this amount. What if your scholarship stipend gets paid to you on conclusion of the programme? How will you manage then? You may return the amount if you do not use it, upon your return from Manchester."

I flew out to Manchester with everyone's blessings. I had to live up to everyone's expectations from me. I gave my everything to my studies.

CHAPTER TWENTY-FOUR

About MBS and my batchmates

One month at MBS was educative, enlightening and entertaining too. We had excellent Faculty, comfortable stay arrangements and a very well-equipped library. The best part of the programme was the batch. My batchmates 7 in all were the most wonderful people I had met. We all gelled beautifully from the very start. Mark and John were from UK, Costas from Cyprus, Mary from Ireland, and Suresh, Soumitra, Somdeb and I from India.

The Business School indulged us a lot. We had an exclusive dining room to ourselves with the most dainty dishes and wines being served at every meal. We were given passes to the Manchester Y Club and taxis would ferry us to the club each morning.

One weekend, the Business School organised to take us to Chester and we were driven there in a long limousine. Then on another evening, Pikay, one of our Faculty members, gave us a tour of Manchester, sharing with us the history of places that he took us to.

CHAPTER TWENTY-FIVE

Mary in a saree at dinner

We were allowed to bring guests to one evening dinner. That evening Mary and I had a super surprise for all the guys in our batch.

Mary was always in awe of the saree that I had once worn in the programme. She wanted to wear one too. So that evening I draped a saree for Mary and she looked so stunning! What a transformation too! With all the Indian accessories of a bindi (a red vermilion dot on the forehead), long earrings and glass bangles, it was difficult to tell that this was our Mary. We decided to play a prank on the guys.

As Mary and I entered the dining hall, the guys were simply struck by the charming beauty of Mary. No one recognised her as Mary and I introduced her as my college friend. All missed Mary at the dinner, wondering why she hadn't joined us. It was only after the dinner was over that Mary and I let her real identity known. I think what followed must be some of the most unforgettable moments for our Mary. The shower of compliments she received was simply overwhelming!

CHAPTER TWENTY-SIX

Prank on Ali

Though the course at MBS was only one month, the bonds that we built with our teachers and batchmates were lifelong.

In each class, we had to sit with our name tent card placed in front of us. The Faculty would read our tent cards and then call out our names. After 2 weeks we thought of checking one of our teacher's memory. Just before our Faculty for Finance, Ali entered the class, we quickly jumbled up all the tent cards and sat down with straight faces hoping no one's face gave away our little prank. We intended to confuse the Faculty.

Ali entered the class and in his inimitable style started teaching the subject. In a short span of 2 weeks, we had already grown very fond of him. That day, Ali would pose a question to the open class and then go up to individual participants seeking the answer. He would call out the correct name of that participant regardless of the tent card he/she was displaying. We realised that Ali already knew our names and that he really did not need to see our tent cards when referring to us in class.

This went on with Ali enjoying his little game until he came up to me and posed a question saying "Yes John, will you give me the answer?" I thought that if he could not remember my name at least he shouldn't mix me up with John. Clearly John was a guy's name and I was a lady. I looked at Ali indignantly and he kept repeating "Yes John, what is your answer?" Then he slowly turned my tent card inwards and I read John on it. In all the scramble to interchange the cards before Ali entered the class, I was sitting with John's card. The joke was on us!!

When we finally had to part after 1 month together, it was not easy. My teacher Pikay and my batchmates dropped me at the Manchester airport from where I flew back to Mumbai, India.

CHAPTER TWENTY-SEVEN

Sharing MBS learning with my senior

Once back in the office, it felt like a homecoming. My senior, Mr.Syamal Gupta, welcomed me back very warmly and we got down to work immediately. I was eager to share with him, all the learning that I had brought back. A week went past and I was still waiting for Mr. Gupta to ask me to share with him, my take-home from the MBS programme.

On Day 7 of my return at around 3 p.m. I saw the door to his chamber opening. He appeared to be in a hurry to leave for an appointment. I thought if he leaves now then it would be one more day gone without him asking me share what I had brought back. I began to think that it really did not matter to him whether I had gone or not gone to this course! I needed to make it matter to him and I needed to make it matter to him now, I resolved.

Thinking thus I went to him saying "It is 7 days today that I am back from MBS and you have not asked me even once what I studied there and how I would want to apply that learning here. I have decided that I am not going to wait any longer for you to ask me. I am going to tell you and I will do it right now." Not showing any displeasure at my small outburst, he very humbly pleaded, "Please you have to let me go. I have a meeting with the Group Chairman and I cannot be late for that. If you let me go now, I promise to come back and listen to everything you have to share." Notice the humility of this senior! As if I was in any position to hold him back! Yet here he was standing there and talking so humbly and pleading with me to let him go. "I shall be waiting" I said, sounding as if I were his grandmother.

Our office was mid-town and Group Chairman's office was downtown. Mr. Gupta's house too was downtown. I thought the meeting with the Group Chairman would end well past closing time so Mr. Gupta would prefer to go home instead of coming way out, back to the office. Office closed at 5.15 p.m. I waited.

At 7 p.m. Mr. Gupta walked in gesturing me to join him in his room. He said, "Come my child, my time now is entirely yours." Starting that day, from 7 p.m. to 10 p.m. for the next 30 days, we sat together discussing my learning of 30 days that I spent in Manchester. I treasured these hours and used to look forward to 7 p.m. each evening. He had so many questions to ask. Questions that made me think, reason and analyse and I could feel my learning from MBS was now finally coming home to me.

Yet my biggest learning was to come when we were discussing Day 13 of the course. That was the day at the SEC programme when we had developed a leadership model of 4 quadrants and we were asked to place our boss in one of the quadrants. "That's me. Where did you place me?" He asked. I pointed out one of the quadrants. He was shocked. "But that is where you would place the poorest kind of a leader. You put me there? Obviously, you have some very strong reasons for putting me there. Can you give me some examples of my behaviour that made you place me in this quadrant?"

I went about heartlessly pointing out 3 to 4 instances of me observing his interaction with other managers in the office in the recent past, which I thought should have been otherwise different.

He listened without interruption. At the end of it, all he said was,

"Is this how I appear to you all? I am so sorry, that is not my intention." That was the only day when we closed our sharing session early, for he said he wanted to go home and mull over what I had said. "You have given me much to think over today," he said.

Today when I train corporate leaders in giving and receiving feedback, this is one instance I always narrate. The way I gave feedback is exactly what I tell my participants not to do and the extremely mature manner, the humility, the openness with which he accepted the feedback was way beyond any ordinary person's capacity to accept negative feedback being hurled at him in so heartless a manner.

Obviously, I was not working with an ordinary leader. He was far too extra-ordinary in every way. My small egoistic self, at that point in time, had failed to notice his greatness.

With great patience, he was moulding me, investing in me and shaping me into a better person. Truly a guru in every way. To think I had the audacity to place him in the lowest quadrant of the model! It was really my inability to see greatness in others that made me foolishly do that.

There is so much to learn from others around us and why would they invest so much of their time and energy? What do they gain? Why do they do this? Great leaders do this because they love their juniors and want to give them the opportunity to rise above the ordinary. I have been very blessed in life to be able to learn at the feet of such great gurus.

Needless to say that inspite of my so called "enjoyable fights" with Mr. Gupta, (which he enjoyed but which always left me infuriated,) never once was he vindictive. Neither did he ever demonstrate ego and pull me up when I used an angry tone with him. In fact each encounter, I think, was fun for him. He was slowly and surely grooming me all along.

CHAPTER TWENTY-EIGHT

Tea with Mr. Palkhivala

My thoughts fly back to the time I was privileged to spend with some of the finest human beings the Lord has created. One amongst them was also Mr. Nani Palkhivala. Soft-spoken and humble, a stalwart of a person.

When I was working with Tata International Limited, Mr.Palkhivala was the Chairman of the company. Sometimes he would invite me to have tea with him at 4 p.m. in his office at Bombay House. Bombay House is the corporate headquarters of the Tata Group. When I first stepped into Mr. Palkhivala's office, I found myself in a big, tastefully done up room with a large table and seated behind the big desk was Mr. Palkhivala. He appeared so small and sweet. "You look so small sitting behind such a large desk" I exclaimed.

"So kind of the Tatas to give me such a big office and such a large desk," was his humble response. Humility is the hallmark of great individuals, and here I was standing in front of someone who was humility personified. For all his achievements and his intellectual genius Mr. Palkhivala remained the most humble and loving person that I have ever come across.

CHAPTER TWENTY-NINE

Jetlag

A jewel of a human being, Mr. Syamal Gupta was someone who had dedicated his life to the Tata Group. When I worked closely with him, I noticed that regardless of any time zone that he may have travelled to, Mr. Gupta would always come straight to the office from the airport. I wondered why inspite of being so much younger than him, did I need to go home to sleep off jetlag. So the next time when I returned from one of my trips abroad, I went straight to the office.

By late afternoon, my head was groggy and there was poor coordination between my words and actions.
I answered a call from Mr.Palkhivala. He was looking for some details. I offered to give them to him right away. Instead of passing on the details to him, I hung up the call. Mr.Palkhivala called again and I repeated the act. Mr.Palkhivala called a third time, this time enquiring if I was okay for he said I did not appear the sort of a person to him, who would hang up on anyone. I explained how I had made a mistake that day in trying to mimic Mr. Gupta's act and how I was messing up all my work and ending up wasting other people's time as well.

Very sweetly he said, "I suggest you go home and rest my dear." That's it. No show of irritation or anger. No ego whatsoever. Mr.Palkhivala's words were always laced with lots of love whenever he spoke. Where there is love, ego, anger and irritation have no place.

CHAPTER THIRTY

Invitation to B. D. Goenka awards ceremony

When I was working with Tata BP in Bangalore, I received an invitation to attend the B.D. Goenka awards for journalism. I did not have anything to do with journalism nor did I know any journalists. I was not aware as to who had sent me the invitation. Nonetheless I decided to attend the function.

Bangalore those days was known as the retired men's paradise. After 7 p.m. you would not see anyone on the streets. Since the award function was to close at 8 p.m. one of my colleagues offered to come with me and later drop me home.

We reached Hotel Ashoka, the venue of the awards function at 4 p.m. It was a pleasant surprise to see Mr.Palkhivala there. He greeted me very lovingly and thanked me for having accepted his invitation to the function. I learnt that Mr. Palkhivala was the Chairman of the awards committee and he was to chair that evening's function.

During the break, Mr. Palkhivala came up to me saying, "Wait after the function. I will drop you home. I do not want you to be going alone at that hour." Mr. Palkhivala was staying in Hotel Ashoka itself. I thanked him and introduced him to my colleague and told him that my colleague would drop me home. "Thank-you for offering to drop my child home," Mr. Palkhivala said to my colleague.

Mr. Palkhivala was always full of love for all around him. It was impossible to be in his company and not be enveloped in the warmth of his love and understanding.

• 52 •

CHAPTER THIRTY-ONE

Marketing brochures

In teams there are bound to be differences of opinion. And there should be differences because it is healthy to have different points of view to any situation. Shouting, screaming, raising voices at the place of work achieve nothing. They only create bad vibrations and ruin everyone's health. In one of the companies, I worked with, there prevailed a culture of "Boss's voice the loudest". No mistakes were tolerated. The result was more mistakes by nervous employees.

One evening we received new marketing brochures from our marketing agency. I requested my department's secretary to mail them to all our dealers with a personal note signed by him. A week later, this secretary who had been at the receiving end of the boss's wrath, far too often, came up to me with his closest all-time companion. This closest all-time companion was his handkerchief, which he pulled out umpteen times in a day to dab off his perspiration, each time he got shouted at.

He stood at my desk wiping his brow again and again. I noticed he was hiding something behind his back. I thought if I ignore him for some time he will settle down. When his nervousness showed no signs of ebbing, I asked him, "Come on my friend, please tell me why you are here and what is it that you are hiding behind your back."

"You will shout if I show you" was his tension-ridden response.

"I am not the shouting-screaming sort. The day I shout at you, please remember that there is nothing wrong with you but something is wrong with me. And if I shout, you shout back, OK! Now will you show me?"

"How can I shout at you?" he squeaked.

"So how can I too shout at you?" I squeaked mimicking his tone.

He slowly extended his hand to show me the letter he had received from one of the dealers. The dealer had written that he had received only the covering letter, but no brochures were attached.

"My God! You wasted so much of your perspiration for this! Please write back apologising for the oversight and send him the brochures. No big deal" was my response to the whole situation.

"So, you are not going to shout?" Poor fellow was so used to being fired all the time that he could not believe that he was not on the firing line with me.

How could I forget how I was moulded and how all my mistakes were overlooked when I was on the learning curve?

This young boy soon rose to assume higher roles in the Exports division of the company.

CHAPTER THIRTY-TWO

Sunil's story

My last assignment as an employee of the Tata group was to set up the Human Resource Department in Tata International Limited. I was to report to the new Managing Director, Mr. Sudhir Deoras.

Mr. Sudhir Deoras called in the Head of Personnel and told him to give me one person from his team as I would need at least one person to help me. Instantly the Head of Personnel responded "Give her Sunil (name changed). His gestures showed as if he was wanting to rid himself of Sunil. Mr. Deoras asked me if looking at the manner in which Sunil was being offered to me, did I still want to team up with him. My answer was affirmative.

As we moved out of the Managing Director's room, the Head of Personnel explained that Sunil had been in the company for 10 years and that I would be his 9th boss. He mentioned that Sunil was bone-lazy and that his output was one big zero. However, Sunil had a fantastic knack of appearing very busy whole day long.

It did not take long to discover that Sunil had been through a whole lot of adverse situations at work. Sunil had been offered a job in the Company at the demise of his father who was in the company's service. This young college boy suddenly had to face traumatic situations at home and work. At work, no one ever took the efforts to show him the job. He would be assigned a job but never taught how it was meant to be done and then when he floundered over it, the job would be taken away from him and assigned to someone else. In the process Sunil's output was seen to be as "one big zero".

Soon Sunil and I became the HR team of the company. Sunil was intelligent and enthusiastic. Circumstances had made him bitter and uncooperative. In the very first year of our working together, Sunil emerged as a star in the annual appraisal. Sunil and I enjoyed working together and soon we were setting up world class HR systems in the Company.

CHAPTER THIRTY-THREE

Going to Dewas

Sunil had great organising capability. Once about 30 of us from Mumbai were to travel to Dewas for a training programme organised internally by HR. I was one of the 30. Sunil put me totally at ease saying that I should not worry about any organising as he had taken care of everything. He was not a part of the group of 30. He had assigned duties to the young management trainees in the group to take care of all arrangements during our overnight train journey. The tickets were handed over to one of the management trainees, the money to buy dinner for the group from the pantry car was given to another. The third management trainee was assigned the task of looking after the Programme Faculty's comfort. The Programme Faculty was a teaching member of a reputed management school and was to board the train at the starting point along with us. "Everything is taken care of. You simply relax and enjoy the programme Kamal," my Sunil told me, as all of us were leaving the office to go to the railway station, that evening. I was very impressed.

The journey was very eventful. The Programme Faculty did not show up and the train started. There was no pantry car on the train and we had 30 people to serve dinner to. None of us carried drinking water either. Eventually everything ironed out and we returned having had a great learning experience after 5 days of intense training.

Sunil was eagerly awaiting feedback from me on his arrangements and as I narrated everything to him, we couldn't stop laughing about all the funny adjustments that the management trainees made to the seemingly flawless arrangements by Sunil. That one journey taught us back-up planning for life! All the fun way!

Each new assignment made Sunil shine forth. Whether he learnt while doing a job or he learnt through mistakes, Sunil was learning, growing and glowing. Her was our bright star! His enthusiasm was contagious too.

Sunil today heads the Human Resource function for a group of companies spread across the globe.

CHAPTER THIRTY-FOUR

Vimal and Anil did not get along

There are times when however much we try, we simply cannot bring ourselves to love some people.

One such pair was Anil and Vimal (both names changed). Anil was located at our Delhi office and Vimal at Mumbai. Both had served the organisation very well, for quite a few years. Both were good in their work, but both could not stand the sound of each other. There were no cell phones at that time. The two had never met but when we saw Vimal talking in a very high-pitched tone on the phone at Mumbai office, we could tell that Anil in Delhi was at the receiving end. Perhaps Anil was doing the same at his end too.

Sunil and I decided to put Anil and Vimal together in the same room for the entire duration of the training programme in Dewas, that we just referred to. The Mumbai group reached the venue and settled into their rooms. The Delhi group was to arrive soon. Vimal learnt that his room partner for the next 5 days was to be Anil. This was simply unacceptable to him. How can HR (which was Sunil and I) make such a blunder!

Vimal came rushing to me saying "Kamal, please quickly change Anil's room. Get anyone else to share my room with me. You know Anil is a very disliked person, so I suggest you leave him in a separate room by himself for nobody will be happy sharing the room with him!" Had Delhi group arrived before Mumbai group, perhaps Anil would have had similar things to say about Vimal.

I explained to Vimal that change in rooms was not possible and when he got to see Anil for the first time, if he disliked the look of him too, then he could stay away from him and use the room only after Anil had slept off. Vimal was most upset with me but there was no alternative available to him.

I do not know what the first meeting between the two was like, but after 5 days when it was time to return to Delhi/Mumbai, we saw the two hugging each other, promising full support to each other at work and even inviting each other to their respective cities for a holiday with family!

This miraculous change in both our colleagues was much talked about in Delhi and Mumbai offices and as Sunil puts it, it was "the biggest achievement of HR at team building!"

Love conquers all! Love brings understanding along with it. Where there is love, there is no room for misunderstanding.

CHAPTER THIRTY-FIVE

Japanese bow

Once I was to travel for work to Japan. I was then working with Mr.Syamal Gupta. Mr.Gupta had returned from Tokyo a month before I was to travel. He insisted that I learn the Japanese language before departing for Tokyo as he felt that would be an advantage. We organised a Japanese language teacher with help from the Japanese Consulate. A few of us from the office opted for the course.

While the language training was on, Mr.Gupta took it upon himself to teach me business etiquette typical to the Japanese. A good learning was that the Japanese are very punctual. Be it for business meetings or for social dinners.

One day he decided to train me in the Japanese way of greeting people, the bow. I asked him how low I was supposed to bend. He thought it over a few seconds and then suggested that I observe the greeting being exchanged between him and the visitor from Mitsubishi that afternoon in the office.

What happened that afternoon was hilarious. When the Japanese officer from Mitsubishi arrived, he greeted Mr. Gupta with a bow. Mr.Gupta bowed in return, only he bowed lower than what our visitor had done. The visitor bowed back, lower than what Mr.Gupta did followed by Mr.Gupta and again the visitor. Amused by what I was observing, I wondered if it would stop only with someone hitting his head on the ground.

After the meeting, in a pretty matter of fact tone Mr.Gupta said, "Now you know how much to bow!"

When I recounted my observations laughing at what I saw, he said, "Then you better check this out with your Japanese teacher." I am glad I did. There is an etiquette to it based on the level of seniority of the 2 people greeting each other. Had I gone purely by Mr.Gupta's teaching, I would have ended up being the laughing stock for the Japanese, though of course they are too polite to let their visitor even know that the visitor is making a faux pass.

CHAPTER THIRTY-SIX

Sushi

Etiquette is nothing but an expression of love and understanding. Concern for the other person is what it is all about. Mr. Gupta always used to say, "Never let your hosts ever feel embarrassed."

While in Tokyo, one evening one of the Directors of Mitsubishi hosted a dinner at the Mitsubishi club for my 2 colleagues and me, the 3-member delegation from Tata International Limited.

Much before we left for Tokyo, Mitsubishi had enquired if we would like to try some Sushi. Being a vegetarian, I had declined but my 2 colleagues had shown eagerness to taste it. So, at this dinner Mitsubishi served Sushi to my colleagues. They explained that Sushi was a Japanese delicacy which was served only on special occasions to very special guests. We felt honoured and thanked our hosts.

That night both my colleagues faced severe reaction in their bodies due to the Sushi they had relished at the dinner. The next night another Director from Mitsubishi hosted the dinner in our honour and Sushi was served. Not wanting to embarrass the hosts, my 2 colleagues ate the Sushi served to them and suffered the same after-effects the second night in a row.

Unfortunately, we had a repeat of this on the third night as well but my colleagues never let their discomfort known to the hosts.

CHAPTER THIRTY-SEVEN

Fridge in Tokyo

In my endeavour to inculcate within myself, the 5 basic human values, I opted for love. Sure enough all my life I saw that the more I shared love the more I received it, often from unexpected sources too. Love expresses itself in many forms. Understanding, respect and concern for others are but a few of these forms.

When I opened the refrigerator in my tiny matchbox room in the hotel in Tokyo, I found that it looked different. It had tiny bottles of all shapes hanging from clamps of different sizes. I pulled out one cute little bottle. It turned out to be a liquor bottle. To my horror, I heard the clanging as if some coins were dropping in a metal box.

I then noticed a sign, placed on the refrigerator saying that anything pulled out from the refrigerator would automatically be added to the hotel bill downstairs. I did not drink neither did I have any intention of consuming any liquor.

Everything in Japan was frightfully expensive too. I did not want my company to pay for my mistake. I called the billing counter and explained how my curiosity had got me into this problem and I certainly did not want to consume it nor did I want my company to be billed for it.

I had decided that if the hotel insisted on payment, which they could have because they had placed the sign on the refrigerator which I read only eventually, then I would pay up from my personal funds, but certainly not allow my company to take the tab for my mistake.

The billing staff was very understanding and waived that amount.

CHAPTER THIRTY-EIGHT

Room in Bangkok

On my way back from Tokyo, I had stopped in Bangkok for business for 2 days. My room in Bangkok appeared palatial and huge. I almost felt guilty to make my company pay for such a big room for just 2 nights.

When I called reception asking for a smaller room, I was told this was a standard size room and since I was coming from Tokyo, any room would now feel too large.

Love overflows

Wherever life has taken me, I have always found myself surrounded by love. When I was transferred to Tata BP Solar, Bangalore, for the first few weeks I stayed in the company's guest house, until I moved into my rented house. The CEO of the company, Mr. A K Vora, occupied the apartment adjoining the company's guest house.

When Mrs. Vora learnt that I could not consume any oily or spicy food because of a liver ailment, she took it on to herself to make idlis, dosas and all kinds of food that I could manage to eat.

All of us can contribute much more at work when the atmosphere is permeated with love. In this case that love extended even to the CEO's house!

CHAPTER FORTY

Buddha Baba

Sometimes we come across some people who find it difficult to express warmth. Does that mean that they are bereft of any feeling of love? Actually No. They do express at the appropriate time and we have to be alert to spot it and feel it. If we start writing off such people, we will always be left starving for their warmth.

That reminds me of an old beggar on the streets of Bangalore. Every morning I had to walk down one street to reach the pick-up point for my office van. On the way was a church and across the church used to be a street-side tea vendor. As I walked past each morning, I used to observe a hunched up old man sitting on the cold stone floor just inside the gate of the church. He had a small begging bowl placed near him. Now and then I used to put a coin in his bowl.

Winter in Bangalore was cold. Those days we Mumbai residents never owned a sweater for we did not have a cold winter in Mumbai. However, it was 9 degrees and below in Bangalore and I used to find it very cold.

One morning I sat down in front of the old beggar man and asked him if he would like a warm cup of tea. The floor he was sitting upon was made of stone and the stone could really get cold. I used to call the beggar man "Buddha Baba" meaning "elderly father". Buddha Baba sat huddled up in an oversized suit jacket that someone must have given him. His face was not visible. He did not respond to me. I left a few coins with the tea vendor requesting him to serve a hot cup of tea to Buddha Baba. I had to rush lest I miss my company transport. This became a daily ritual. Buddha Baba would never talk to me, and I never got to see his face.

One morning I had requested my colleagues travelling with me on the office van to skip my regular pick-up point and to pick me up from the next pick-up point as I had stayed over with some family friends the previous night. When the van arrived to pick me up, I asked them why they were late and they said it was because of my Buddha Baba.

It seems that when Buddha Baba saw that our office van was leaving from my regular pick-up point without me, Buddha Baba rushed and blocked the road standing in front of the van. He refused to let the van go saying, I must have been delayed that morning, but they should wait and not leave without taking "his daughter" with them.

We do not know from where the shower of love will fall upon us each day. Give an ounce, receive in tons!

CHAPTER FORTY-ONE

Billing not done for Tata companies

When I quit my job after 10 years with the Tata group and started corporate training, I never would bill a Tata company for the work I did for them. One year down the line Mr. Syamal Gupta, discovered this and he pulled me up saying "We do not want you to work for free. If you say that this is your gurukul and you learnt everything from here, then stand up and train many more in what you have gained, give back much more."

Even after more than 20 years of quitting as an employee of the Tata group, I still refer to it as "my group".

I have received so much love from everyone in the Tata group that I do not think even if I train day and night I could give back what I have received.

CHAPTER FORTY-TWO

Starting on my own

When I was passing out of my MBA, my career goal was very clear – I wanted to be a Corporate Trainer running a training firm of my own. To be able to do proper justice to my work, I needed cross-functional exposure in the corporate world. My teachers at NMIMS told me that I should be joining the Tata Group. "No one trains like the Tatas," they said.

When I joined Tata Exports I had let my career goal known to them. Tatas, true to their word gave me tremendous cross-functional exposure within the Group, allowing me to move within the group companies. Added to this, was also wide international exposure.

My plan was to start off on my own 10 years after my MBA. 10 years were coming to a close. It was not an easy decision to take, to move on. I was doing very well in the Tata Group. I was much appreciated. I was enveloped with love. I had grown very fast and there remained new heights to scale.

It was the renowned Indian Cricketer, Mr. Vijay Merchant who always used to say, "When you have to give up something in life and move on, do so when people ask *Why* and not *Why not.*"

My eldest sister who lives in the USA was visiting us. She enquired what my plans were, now that 10 years were coming to a close. I shared that I had certain commitments due to which

I was hesitating. She, very sweetly helped me find my solutions and got me started.

In August 2000, I finally put my pen down as a Tata employee after 10 wonderful years with my Group. This Group brought into my life, some of the most beautiful people, I was blessed to meet and to work with. The Tata Group gave me the kind of friends with whom my bonds are lifelong, for these are bonds of love. And true enough, till date even though it is over 20 years after I have moved on, the bonds of love are just as strong.

There are trainers and trainers out there. How will you be different

When I decided to move on to start a corporate training firm of my own, Mr. Syamal Gupta had asked me, "There are trainers and trainers out there. How will you be different?"

He went on to tell me "Stay with your clients long enough to see the results of your training." It is this advice that my team and I have followed all throughout these 20 odd years.

It is so satisfying to see the results come in. Each set of participants has gone back and implemented the learning. Our joy doubles when we learn that our participants and their organisations are doing well. Batch after batch that we train does us proud. We feel so blessed.

CHAPTER FORTY-FOUR

How I got started

As mentioned earlier, the last assignment that I completed with the Tata Group as an employee of the Group, was to set up the HR department in Tata International Limited.

One afternoon when I was at my desk, a young management trainee from another Tata Group company came up to me requesting for a ride to the Taj Hotel where both of us were scheduled to attend the same meeting.

I was happy to have company while driving down from my office to the Taj. On the way this young girl started weeping. I realised she needed to talk. I parked by the side of the road and heard her out. She was facing some nasty problems at work and did not know how to handle those. I talked her through and helped her arrive at her solutions. I think she felt better.

The very next day after I quit the Tata Group to start on my own, I was pleasantly surprised to receive a call from this young lady. She said she was working with BASF in the Learning & Development (L&D) department and had learnt that I was now on my own, wanting to contribute to the area of L&D. She invited me to her office. When we met, she put her annual training calendar in my hands and asked me to take a pick of the programmes that I would like to run for her company, And that's how I got started!

CHAPTER FORTY-FIVE

Unable to get along with lady colleagues

Years have rolled past since I started working with my own 2 firms. The satisfaction my team and I derive from our work is immense. We know that the major reason behind this is the bond that develops between our participants and us. I often used to wonder why participants who did not know me before that 1st day of the programme would seek me out, post training hours and want to discuss their personal problems with me. We have had many such experiences at every programme.

I was once running a 3 days' residential programme for one of my Tata Group companies. Most of my programmes were residential programmes. At this programme, I had 3 lady participants out of a total of 17. On the first day of the programme, my participants and I met for the first time. None of them was known to me before this day.

I noticed in course of the day that one gentleman was not particularly pleasant with the lady participants. If any lady made any contribution at the programme, this gentleman would immediately have a sarcastic comment for that. I could feel the under-currents in the room between the participants. When training for the first day ended, the participants all moved out of the training area towards the residential area. One participant, a lady, was still hanging around as I was packing my laptop and training kit. She said she wanted to speak to me alone.

We sat outside on the steps leading to the training centre. She told me that this gentleman, whom she said I too would have noticed for his rude behaviour towards ladies, was her boss at work. She mentioned he was very nasty and that he would put up his mean exterior only with ladies.

Just then she spotted this gentleman walking up and down on the lawns behind where we were seated. This got her very scared. "Now that he has seen me talking to you alone, he will want to meet you to find out what our discussion was about. He will take it out on me at work. What shall I do now?"

I turned behind waved out to this gentleman and asked loudly, "Hi, are you waiting to speak to me?" He responded in the affirmative.

"I am just about to move to the residential area. Shall we meet there post dinner?" I asked. He agreed and moved away. But the lady was too scared to be seen with me alone any longer, so she chose to close the conversation right there.

Post dinner, as agreed, that gentleman and I put out chairs on the lawns outside our rooms and sat down under a starlit sky. For quite some time that gentleman (let's call him Suraj for the sake of this incident) sat staring at the grass between his 2 feet. I waited patiently for him to begin. When I saw that he was finding it difficult to voice his pain, I broke the silence, "Suraj, you wanted to talk," I said. He chose to remain silent.

"Do you want me to start?" I asked. He looked up at me puzzled. His eyes were asking me, "How do you know what I want to talk to you about?" I slowly responded, "Suraj, I can understand that there is a problem at home, and it involves a lady." To this, he burst out crying. I allowed him to get over his emotions.

Then he spoke, "I was brought up by a single parent, my mother. I lost my father very young. My mother struggled to bring me up, educate me and make me the successful engineer that I am today. My wife too is a very good engineer doing very well in her organisation. She is also much appreciated by her seniors. Unfortunately, my wife and my mother have never got along. On most occasions it was my mother who was at fault but for the sake of peace in the house, my wife and I would always say sorry to her."

After a short pause he continued, "One day matters came to a head and my wife could take it no longer. She was very firm when she told me that I had to now choose between my mother and her and if she left, she would take our 8-year-old daughter with her."

Suraj went on to say that he tried to explain to his wife that he could not abandon his mother at this age when she needed looking after and that he could not be an ungrateful son. Without giving him an opportunity to say anything further, misunderstanding that he was choosing his mother over her, his wife walked out with his daughter. Sobbing heavily he continued, "I love my wife and my daughter and I miss them but my wife refuses to take my calls. She does not allow my daughter to speak with me." Having concluded his part of the story, Suraj fell back silent.

Luckily for us, on that day of the programme, we had worked on our inter-personal skills. I asked Suraj if what we had learnt in course of the day, could also be applied to our personal lives and he responded in the affirmative. We decided to choose only 2 lessons and to implement those right away.

It was so heart-warming to receive an email message from Suraj, exactly 7 days after we returned home from the programme, saying his wife and he were together again.

All that we shared in the Inter-personal skills module were the profound messages of 'Love all, Serve all, Help ever, Hurt never'.

I learnt that Suraj had also started reaching out to all his colleagues at work and that now he was so much easier to work with too.

CHAPTER FORTY-SIX

Slip disc and hard wooden chair

Two months after a Leadership Development Programme in Voltas, one of our participants had this experience to share.

He told us that he suffered from slip disc and was advised 1 month bed rest. He had to sleep on a hard wooden bed. Later when it was time for him to resume work, He was worried about recurrence of that excruciating pain because he could not manage to sit on cushioned chair in the office. He needed a hard wooden chair.

The day he resumed work, he was pleasantly surprised to see a hard wooden chair placed at his desk. Those days a wooden chair was difficult to come by but his thoughtful colleagues had located one and kept it ready. "Why did I lose so much sleep last night worrying about a chair! I am so blessed to have such caring colleagues at work," he thought.

When he thanked his departmental colleagues, he was told "We simply followed the lessons of Love all, Serve all and Help Ever which Kamal had shared with us."

CHAPTER FORTY-SEVEN

The broken laptop

It is one thing to talk and another to implement. My team and I have this one rule amongst ourselves, which we strictly adhere to. We would not speak on anything, which we had not ourselves implemented first.

Once I was running a session at Tata Power on Inter-personal skills. The arrangement of the laptop and other equipment was such that the cables were running across the floor over quite a distance.

In the afternoon the participants chose to have tea served at their seats. When the canteen boy tried to serve me tea by reaching for the speaker's table, he tripped over my laptop cable. The laptop was thrown off the table with great force and it landed on the floor in pieces. My immediate reaction was to run up to the canteen boy to check if he was alright. Once assured that he was unhurt, I apologised to my participants that for the balance 2 hours' programme of that day, we would have to do without a slide show because the laptop was unusable.

My participants' response took me by surprise. They said no amount of slide show, or my talking would help them sharpen their inter-personal skills any further than what they saw as a positive demonstration of the skills right there in front of their eyes, when not caring about my laptop I chose to instantly run to the canteen boy.

The words of the wise ones rang in my ears "an ounce of practice is worth more than a million words." I could only manage to silently bow down to all those beautiful people in my life who helped bring about that spontaneous reaction in me.

CHAPTER FORTY-EIGHT

Training for an insurance company

I guess when you receive so much you also want to give back much more. When insurance business was privatised in India, I started running a whole lot of training programmes for one of the reputed large insurance companies. I was the only trainer hired from outside. The other trainers running similar training programmes were internal to the company. These internal trainers were young, fresh MBAs with no training experience.

Consistently, ratings by participants at my programmes were way higher than those of the other trainers. These trainers were constantly pulled up very badly, sometimes even in my presence by their HR Head. It was very painful to see how they were being spoken to. I decided that I would help narrow down this gap in ratings. I started calling the other trainers home. I shared with them, my methods and the other training material which I used to make my programmes lively and interesting.

Dog-eat-dog culture helps no one. There is enough room for all who want to deliver quality. Often when we help others, it invariably comes back to us many times more. That is why it is said, "Help as much as you can, as lovingly as you can, and as silently as you can. Do not worry about the result but thank the Lord that he blessed you with an opportunity to help."

CHAPTER FORTY-NINE

MIQ ratings

After running over 30 programmes at Mahindra and Mahindra Limited, I was one day introduced to Mr. Davasia who was at that time the Director of Mahindra Institute of Quality (MIQ).

It was Mr. Davasia's firm belief that the technical training being imparted by MIQ must be laced with training in people skills. Technically sound guys can fail to make an impact if their people skills are poor.

In my first meeting with him, Mr. Davasia very categorically told me that MIQ had a very strict rating process and that every aspect of a training programme and of the Trainer were rated by participants daily for every session of the programme. He said that the highest benchmark achieved at MIQ was 65% and that if I failed to meet this benchmark, MIQ would not be interested in continuing with me.

I completed my first 2-day programme with MIQ and returned home. The next morning I received a call from Mr. Davasia's office requesting me to go across to his office at the earliest.

Once seated across the table, Mr. Davasia (his demeanour appeared softer that day, compared to our first meeting) informed me that the overall rating for my programme had turned out to be 91%. He said that at first he thought there was a mistake somewhere so he got down to studying the individual rating points per session, per day and he found that consistently the rating was above 90%.

Now what do you have to say to this?" He asked. "Given the opportunity to continue to work with MIQ, I shall work at improving the scores," I responded.

What followed was a beautiful association with Mr. Davasia and MIQ. Mr. Davasia would take the pains to give me detailed inputs about every Batch that I addressed at MIQ, thus helping me tailor-make every programme to ensure its success.

Give back to society – The Hermitage EAGLE programme

For a long time, industry had been concerned about the quality of engineers passing out of colleges each year. Managers spent a lot of their working time correcting the email messages drafted by the new engineering recruits. In our leadership development programmes we keep insisting on investing in people. The scene in most of our client companies was similar. Leaders train the younger lot; the younger lot learns and moves on to other companies.

One evening when in the Nani Palkhivala Memorial Lecture at NCPA, Mr. Syamal Gupta, prevailed upon me that I should be considering working directly with colleges to tackle this situation in industry. With the help of Mr. F C Kohli, who needs no intorduction, I got in touch with College of Engineering, Pune (COEP). We got together a group of companies and gathered inputs from the COEP Director, Deans and Heads of Departments. What evolved was The Hermitage EAGLE programme, where EAGLE was the acronym for Energising Accelerated Growth and Leadership Excellence.

All third-year engineering students underwent this 10-month long programme. The programme involved tremendous participation from industry. The Tata Trusts, Tata Consulting Engineers Limited, Kirloskar Brothers Limited and Thermax came forward to sponsor the 1st batch of students under this programme.

Each sponsor worked actively with us, shoulder to shoulder, throughout the 10 months' duration.

This programme was conducted in 3 phases. The first stage the Nurturing stage, of 4 months duration focussed on personal development of the student. The second stage, the Learn to fly stage, helped developing their social skills and the last stage, the Soaring stage, prepared them for their roles in industry.

The Hermitage EAGLE programme became a run-away success.

CHAPTER FIFTY-ONE

Feeding two beggar women

As a part of continuous evaluation process, the Eaglets (that is what we called our participants) had to share with us 2 instances of application of learning each month. The instances shared opened our eyes to a new dimension totally.

Here were 700 youthful energetic students who were being transformed onto mature and understanding leaders of tomorrow. They displayed a superb combination of qualities of the head and heart.

One student wrote that one afternoon when he was having his lunch in the hostel canteen, he noticed the manager of the canteen shooing away 2 beggar women with 2 children. The women were pleading to be fed saying that they were all starving. The manager was shouting for the security guards to take these 4 away. Our Eaglet could not bear to eat another morsel knowing that these 4 had no food in their tummies. He went up to the manager and requested him to feed all 4 as his guests and agreed to take the bill for their meals.

Our Eaglet was not from an affluent background. When we asked him as to how would he pay this additional tab on his mess bill at the end of the month, he was very clear that if he avoided the bus in the evening to his coaching class every day for the next 10 days, he would have saved up, in time to pay his monthly mess bill.

Give back to society much more than what you have taken from it, is common philosophy with all the sponsors of the EAGLE programme. We saw how their act of kindness, was grooming tomorrow's leaders.

CHAPTER FIFTY-TWO

The Push

Another Eaglet of ours was on his way back to college from the hostel after finishing his lunch. The sun was hot above. The road was uphill. He noticed a handicapped person struggling to get his vehicle to take the slope. This Eaglet quietly went up to the handicapped person's vehicle and gave it a push to help it take the initial climb.

The handicapped boy turned around to see where had this unexpected help come from. He flashed a very grateful smile to the Eaglet.

This smile was so beautiful and warm that it touched the heart of the Eaglet. An instant bond of love seemed to have been established between these 2 strangers and just for that smile, the Eaglet pushed the vehicle all the way, right up to his college gate, even though the path later had no incline and was flat.

Truly the EAGLE programme was touching lives to make a difference!

CHAPTER FIFTY-THREE

The harbingers of change

Our chat with the local traffic policeman was very heartening. He told us that our Eaglets (the policeman referred to them as the college kids in white T-shirts because our Eagle shirts with the logos were all white) would be harbingers of change in this world. They would never break any traffic rules and if an error did happen, they would insist on being punished.

Most of our Eaglets expressed that if they did anything dishonest even if it was something very small, then they felt that they were betraying the relationship of love and trust between their Eagle Faculty and them.

Love truly transforms!

CHAPTER FIFTY-FOUR

Our Programme Faculty's love for us

We had a similar experience a few years later.

We were working with a batch of Graduate Engineer Trainees (GETs) in a corporate. Their HR General Manager addressed them one day. He asked them what was the one factor they would attribute to their transformation. Without any hesitation in one voice came the response "Our Programme Faculty's love for us". Our hearts skipped a few beats on hearing this.

This power of ever-flowing love is unfailing.

CHAPTER FIFTY-FIVE

Paying tax

My colleague Mahendra Parab worked in the Accounts Department of Tata International Limited when I was setting up HR in the same company. We both quit the Tata group at about the same time. We both started our own outfits around the same time. I moved on to set up my firm in corporate training and Mahendra Parab started his own Chartered Accountancy practice.

Mahendra used to handle the accounts for my firm. He still does. Each year when it was time to pay Income Tax, we used to feel the pain of giving so much hard-earned money to the government as tax. We would try to find loopholes, discuss those and calculate the amount of tax we would save if we chose to go that way. Then, each would look at the other with a guilty face for each knew that his and her conscience would not permit such an act.

Tax money is not a gift we are giving to the government nor are we obliging the country by paying our taxes. It is a duty we owe to our nation and we must not falter in fulfilling our duty.

Yet, the next year again when it was time to pay tax, we would grumble. We would grumble that in Mumbai, we do not find even a 1 km. stretch anywhere which is free from potholes. We pay tax honestly but why do we not see the benefits of this money coming to us? Then of course we would go and pay what we had to, without taking recourse to any loopholes.

I am so blessed to have Mahendra Parab handling accounts for me. Not only does he keep the accounts perfectly but has built in so much of discipline in my life and has ensured that I go to bed with a clear conscience each night.

It is only when we started working closely with COEP on The Hermitage EAGLE programme, that we saw how the government was doing a great job of educating the children of the poor. A majority of the students in COEP were drawn from economically lower backgrounds. Some of their fathers were construction site labourers, coolies, auto drivers. Parents were struggling to educate their sons and daughters to become engineers. Some of the kids were the first to be passing out as engineers in their villages. Education was heavily subsidised for all these students.

Now we realised that our tax money was not going waste as we had so incorrectly been thinking.

College study tour

Though this book is intended to share some of my innumerable experiences in the corporate world, I am tempted to end with one experience which happened when I was very raw and young, just 22 years of age, a lecturer at a Commerce & Economics college in Mumbai.

After my M.Com. degree, I was teaching undergraduate students for 2 and a half years. I enjoyed every moment of it. My Principal was very encouraging. My college management was very supportive. My colleagues were very protective and patronising for I was the youngest lecturer and my students were the best. When I was teaching the final year students at the degree college level, some of my students turned out to be older than me in age.

I used very unconventional methods of teaching. We had debates, games, stories, role-plays, puppet shows, industrial visits, even large exhibitions. I would once in a year take my students to a hill station close by for 3 days, study in the open, do some projects and present a detailed report to our college Principal upon our return.

On one such trip, I had put up on the notice board, the list of students who would be going with me and some other teachers on the study tour. The Principal had cautioned me about one particular student who was known to be disobedient and defiant. He had prevailed upon me not to take that student along, as he felt that boy would be quite a handful for me to manage. I did not include that boy in my list.

One morning that boy came up to me in the staff room where I was seated all alone. Rolling up his sleeves in a threatening style he asked me why his name was not seen on the study tour list. I was not intimidated by his act or tone and told him that his very demeanour was an answer to his question. He realised this was not going to work with me.

After this he started following me around the college begging me to take him, assuring all the time that he would be a very good boy. I decided that he should be given a chance to improve. So after a few days he and I had a good conversation together and we decided that this student would be allowed to join the study tour.

I could not get a buy-in from the Principal, but finally I agreed to take him on my personal responsibility. My student proved to be an absolute gem. All throughout the 3 days' study tour, this boy was always in the forefront to help all, to organise all sessions to ensure all meals were ready and served on time, that all had eaten and that all were comfortable.

When we returned to the college, the Principal called me to his room. I saw that this student was already present in the Principal's room. I was wondering what was in store for me. "Kamal, what greater certificate do you want? This boy has come up to me today on his own to apologise for his bad behaviour in the college for these past years. When I asked him why this sudden change of heart, he says that it is entirely due to the way you treated him in course of the study tour. He says he received a lot of love and respect and appreciation from you and that made him feel good. He too now wants to be that kind of an individual."

These words of my Principal were the biggest reward I could ever receive and I had only my parents to thank for it. My parents were epitomes of all the 5 human values of truth, righteous conduct, love, peace and non-violence. I never had to look far to find my role models in life.

This student who was older than me in age and was repeatedly failing in each year of college, cleared his degree that year with a first class.

Three years later when I was awaiting my turn for the campus selection interview at a Tata company post my MBA, I ran into this student. He was by then a salesman for fire extinguishers and had come to that Company for business. He happened to know the Administration Manager of that company and offered to put in a word for me with that Manager! Of course I declined his sweet gesture but the glow of love that lit up my heart that day was beyond compare.

Our parents, our colleagues, our seniors, our juniors and society as a whole, all have a big role to play in our personality development. If at the end of it all, we are able to touch lives and make a difference, we have only the Lord to thank for flooding our life with His light flowing into us through all the beautiful people who touched our life.

Epilogue

I once had a vision of the Lord when I saw Him telling me, "I shall do your personality development". How will He do that? I wondered. He sure has His hands full, I thought.

Then one day He again appeared to tell me "Write a book on Corporate Dharma."

I had no clue what to write. For years I floundered not knowing what to write and where to begin. But then He knows when, how and through whom He wants His work done. Once I surrendered to the Lord, He simply took over.

Mr. Syamal Gupta, my guru from my corporate days who continues to inspire me to this day, told me, "Corporate Dharma is all about people. Write about lessons you have learnt from people in your life." Then suddenly everything fell in place and the words kept spilling out of the pen each time I sat down to write.

This whole process of putting this book together made me realise that I still have many more miles to go, before The Lord gets full satisfaction of a job well done, the job that He set out to do, that of my personality development.

www.ingramcontent.com/pod-product-compliance
Lightning Source LLC
Chambersburg PA
CBHW041338120726
48005CB00014B/2308